INCREDIBLE GHOSTS

of the

BIG SUR COAST

(Number two of an INCREDIBLE GHOSTS series)

by
Randall A. Reinstedt

Cover photo shows a portion of the once thriving coastal community of Notley's Landing. See page 22 for additional pictures and page 32 for story. Bancroft Library Collection.

If bookstores in your area do not carry “INCREDIBLE GHOSTS of the BIG SUR COAST”, copies may be obtained by writing to...

GHOST TOWN PUBLICATIONS

P.O. Drawer 5998
Carmel, CA 93921

Other books by Randall A. Reinstedt, offered by Ghost Town Publications, are:

“GHOSTS, BANDITS AND LEGENDS of old Monterey”
“MONTEREY'S MOTHER LODE”
“SHIPWRECKS AND SEA MONSTERS of California's Central Coast”
“TALES, TREASURES AND PIRATES of old Monterey”
“GHOSTLY TALES AND MYSTERIOUS HAPPENINGS of old Monterey”
“WHERE HAVE ALL THE SARDINES GONE?”
“MYSTERIOUS SEA MONSTERS of California's Central Coast”
“INCREDIBLE GHOSTS of old Monterey's HOTEL DEL MONTE”

Second Printing

ISBN 0-933818-08-4
Library of Congress Catalog Card Number: 82-164106

COLOR-AD PRINTERS • MONTEREY

INTRODUCTION

Big Sur is one of the world's most beautiful and unique areas..., an area that boasts awesome mountains, unsurpassed ocean vistas, beautiful valleys, picturesque redwoods, rocky canyons, forgotten cultures, dramatic shipwrecks, bountiful gold mines, hearty pioneers, lost treasures, cliff-clinging roads, proud people and a rich heritage.

This heritage dates back many centuries, back to the days when Indians were the only people who inhabited the land. Included in this Indian culture, and intimately intertwined with the history of Monterey County's rugged Pacific peaks, are numerous tales told by, and associated with, these "first settlers" of the Big Sur coast. These tales tell of such things as a sacred mountain, a cave of death, mysterious gathering places, healing hot springs, chambers of gold, and a tantalizing "lost world".

As time went on, Spanish explorers and men of God came to this wilderness land of majestic mountains and peaceful people. With their arrival they left marks of a new culture and what they thought to be a civilized world on the inhabitants of this untamed territory. These marks were in many forms, including that of the cross... and that of disease! It was the combination of these offerings, brought to Alta (Upper) California by those who were uninvited, that signaled the beginning of the end for the original settlers of this coastal paradise.

The Spanish also left names, among them being "El Pais Grande del Sur", meaning "The Big Country to the South" (south of the Alta California capital community of Monterey and its nearby mission). This name, most pioneer residents agree, was eventually shortened to the familiar Big Sur (Big South) as we know it today, and has become the accepted name for the area they call home. As to where the "Big South" has its boundaries, one can only throw up his hands and exclaim "Quien sabe!" (Who knows). For some, usually those who are passing through and who are unfamiliar with the area, the name

Big Sur means the Pfeiffer Big Sur State Park..., and only the Big Sur park (nestled in the picturesque Big Sur valley). For those at the opposite end of the spectrum, and who are also unfamiliar with the area, Big Sur encompasses all of the land between California's coastal communities of Carmel and Cambria. Somewhere in between these two extremes is the true Big Sur.

For purposes of this publication the author has chosen his own Big Sur boundaries, and refers to the Big Sur coast as the ruggedly beautiful stretch of land between San Jose Creek (to the north and near Point Lobos Reserve) and Salmon Creek (to the south, near the Monterey-San Luis Obispo County line and the remote Santa Lucia mining district of Los Burros).

This stretch of land is thought by many to be the most scenic section of California's lengthy coast, and is said to rival any shoreline in the world for breath-taking vistas and a difficult-to-describe feeling of timelessness. This 71 mile (highway miles) stretch of land is also noted for its unique and colorful history, as well as for a multitude of unique and colorful characters. Finally, and as would be expected from the title of this publication, the legends and lore of this area boast a bountiful collection of ghostly tales and strange happenings..., and the land is blessed with a myriad of haunting mysteries.

It is these ghosts, these mysteries, and these tales of the unexplained that "INCREDIBLE GHOSTS of the BIG SUR COAST" is about. It is hoped by the author that through the stories offered in this work, residents and visitors of Big Sur will be able to appreciate the area, its people, and its unique heritage all the more. It is also hoped that these very same people will look upon this brief book as an added chapter to the colorful history of California's central coast.

As a final introductory comment, the author wishes to state that those who are familiar with his previous works may recognize selected stories and assorted passages from other titles. This duplication was done in an attempt to incorporate many of the fascinating tales and happenings of the Big Sur-Santa Lucia Mountain areas into one publication. It is hoped that the duplications that do exist do not distract from the book, and that the multitude of new stories and never-before-recorded accounts contained in this offering will more than make up for any tales that have previously been printed. In closing, the author also wishes to mention that at various places throughout the text he lists many of the tales that have already been told, and indicates in which source they originally appeared.

With the preceding comments and introductory information in mind, the author wishes to extend to one and all his wishes for an enjoyable journey along California's incredible Big Sur coast.

ACKNOWLEDGEMENTS

As in all works dealing with history and happenings of the strange and unexplained, a vast amount of research is required. This research takes many forms, with much of it involving the seeking out of diaries, scrapbooks, letters, and assorted other documents left by residents of the areas in question. Other information comes from an assortment of publications (newspapers included) that recount happenings of interest. However, regardless of the information derived from the above-mentioned sources, the most valuable, the most enjoyable, and certainly the most rewarding part of the research is in tracking down and getting to know the people of the areas, and in listening to their stories.

It is with these thoughts in mind, while sitting on a Big Sur hillside writing these acknowledgements (soaking up the scenery and thinking about the many people he has talked with, and the experiences he has shared relating to Monterey County's beautiful south coast, including the information he gained while working as a Big Sur park attendant during his college years), that the author became very much aware of the fact that, in an "unofficial" way, the research for this work began many years ago. It was during these long-ago years that his father, A.M. Reinstedt ("Riney" to his friends), was involved in the building of the coast road and was delivering Standard Oil products to the people of the Sur. In turn, as the author grew to adulthood in neighboring Monterey, it was his father who recounted many fascinating stories of the people and of the happenings pertaining to this rugged region. It is with this in mind that this publication is dedicated to Riney, and to his friends of Big Sur..., people who are as much a part of the history of this wilderness land as are the trees and the mountains..., and the stories they share.

Unfortunately, it is impossible to acknowledge all of the individuals who have shared their secrets and their stories (some, of course, in a "secondhand" way), simply because many of the tales were heard in the dim and distant past and long before any names were taken or thoughts were given to a publication of this type. Nevertheless, as with the author's previous works, he feels it would be most unfair to publish this book without at least acknowledging a few of the personalities who have helped along the way. Among these people are: Jessie Sandholdt, Ruby Woicekowski, Elizabeth Sheilds, Wil Goodrich, Emily Brown, Max and Otto Plapp, Myrtle Leaman, Mary Sherman, Fred Sorri, Joe Victorine, John Crisan Jr., Don Howard, Homer Stephens and Ed and Kuniyo Gardien.

As to sources used in the research of the work (other than those mentioned in the text), the following articles, books and newspaper should be acknowledged: "A Short History of Big Sur" by Ronald Bostwick, "Monterey Coast Fifty-Five Years Ago" by Dr. John L.D. Roberts (written in 1941 by "The Father of the Coast Road"), "Begin the Big Sur... at Palo Colorado Canyon" by Charles Mohler, "Carmel Today and Yesterday" by Daisy Bostick, "Sea Bells" by John Fleming Wilson, "Big Sur" by Tomi Kay Lussier, and the Monterey Peninsula Herald newspaper.

While the above-listed sources and people played important parts in the research of this book, the most heartfelt "Thank you!" is reserved for the author's wife Debbie, his son Erick, and his English bulldog Joshua Jonas McCabe. Once again, it was these three who silently suffered through the trials and tribulations of yet another publication.

CONTENTS

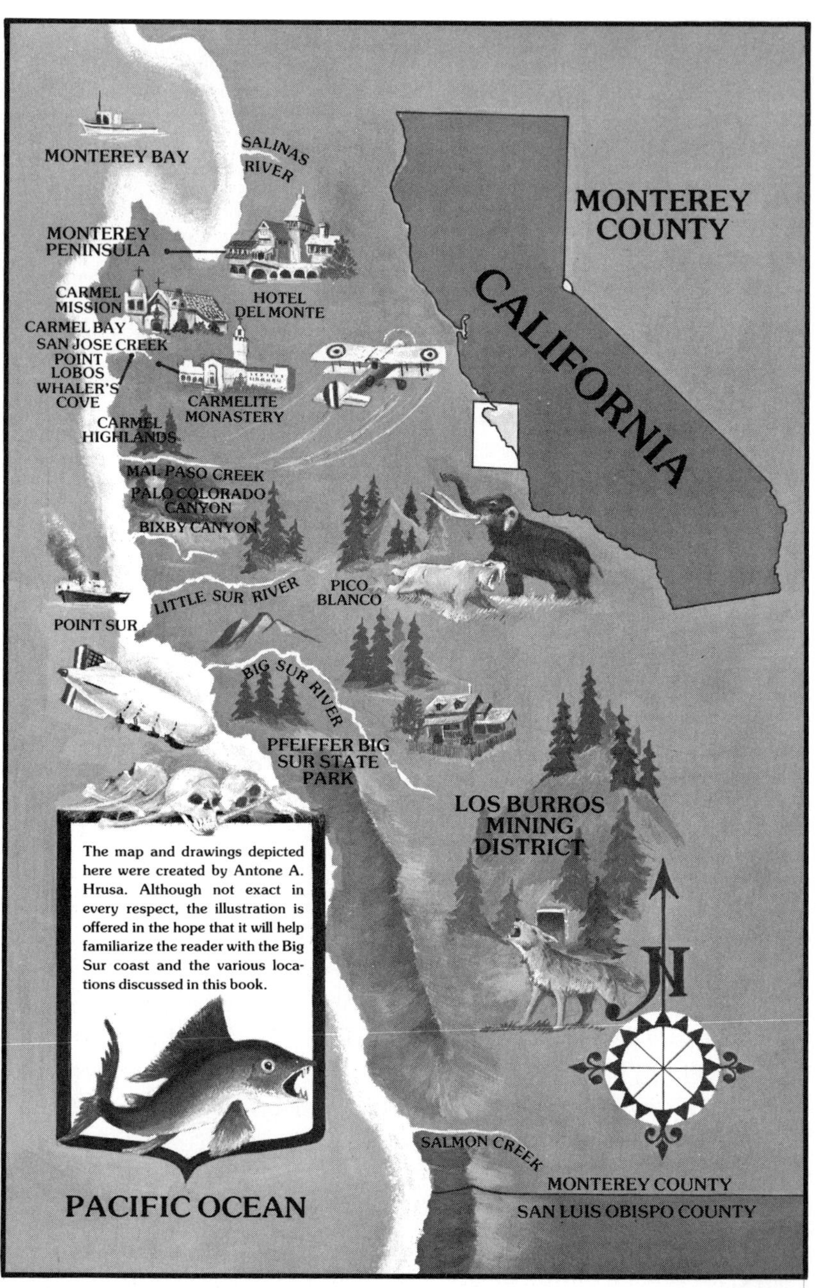
MONTEREY BAY
SALINAS RIVER
MONTEREY COUNTY
CALIFORNIA
MONTEREY PENINSULA
CARMEL MISSION
HOTEL DEL MONTE
CARMEL BAY
SAN JOSE CREEK
POINT LOBOS
WHALER'S COVE
CARMELITE MONASTERY
CARMEL HIGHLANDS
MAL PASO CREEK
PALO COLORADO CANYON
BIXBY CANYON
LITTLE SUR RIVER
PICO BLANCO
POINT SUR
BIG SUR RIVER
PFEIFFER BIG SUR STATE PARK
LOS BURROS MINING DISTRICT
The map and drawings depicted here were created by Antone A. Hrusa. Although not exact in every respect, the illustration is offered in the hope that it will help familiarize the reader with the Big Sur coast and the various locations discussed in this book.
N
SALMON CREEK
MONTEREY COUNTY
SAN LUIS OBISPO COUNTY
PACIFIC OCEAN

INCREDIBLE GHOSTS of the BIG SUR COAST

For purposes of this publication (as previously discussed in the introduction) the Big Sur coast's northern boundary begins at picturesque San Jose Creek. For those unfamiliar with California's Monterey County coast, San Jose Creek is near the beautiful Point Lobos Reserve and is slightly south of the famed Monterey Peninsula (see map, page 8). Those who plan to journey south from the Monterey-Carmel area — whether it be a vicarious trip within the confines of this book, or along the coast's spectacular Highway One — are in for a treat as, with San Jose Creek as a starting point, one of the west's most scenic and interesting areas begins to unfold.

With both the Big Sur coast and this publication having their beginnings along the banks of this Santa Lucia Mountain stream, it should be mentioned that as the text of this book works its way south, and down the rugged Monterey coast, a variety of ghostly occurrences, unexplained happenings, and interesting glimpses into the area's local history will be explored.

As we begin our journey toward the heart of the Big Sur country, it is of interest to note that San Jose Creek winds its way to the sea (Carmel Bay) at a spot known as Monastery Beach (also known as San Jose Creek Beach and part of a coastal stretch that is officially referred to as Carmel River State Beach). It is at Monastery Beach — some say at the mouth of San Jose Creek — that a very steep and extremely deep submarine canyon has its beginning. This canyon is of considerable interest to marine biologists, and it is by following this "Carmel Trench" (as the canyon is sometimes called) toward the shore that many people feel numerous odd and unidentifiable sea beasts have found their way to the waters of Carmel Bay. (For those interested in "local" creatures of the deep, and who wish to learn more about such things, the author's book "MYSTERIOUS SEA MONSTERS of California's Central Coast" contains an abundance of information on marine-oriented oddities of the Big Sur-Monterey Peninsula coasts. See page two for further information).

In getting back to San Jose Creek and Monastery Beach, and in leading up to a story more in keeping with the subject matter of this work, it should be noted that those who follow Highway One south (and away from the Monterey Peninsula) will have no trouble finding beautiful Monastery Beach. Located in a pastoral setting on the Santa Lucia side of the road, and almost impossible to miss for daytime travelers, is the imposing Carmelite Monastery. It is from this striking, red-tiled roof structure that the nearby beach gains its name. Built a half-century ago, this monument to God, and to the Carmelite nuns who reside within, overlooks Carmel Bay and is situated along the banks of San Jose Creek. Opening its doors in 1931, and long before Highway One was completed, the Mediterranean-style structure has graced the landscape for longer than most residents can remember, and today is considered a unique part of the history of the area.

Across the creek and on a neighboring hill is a second site of importance..., a site that takes us considerably further back into local history than either the construction of Highway One or of the opening of the Carmelite Monastery. Discovered in 1968 by a well-known Monterey Peninsula archeologist, the site is that of an ancient Indian village. The village is officially known as "Ichxenta-ruc", but is more commonly referred to as "The Lost Village of San Jose". Its close proximity to San Jose Creek, and the fact that its exact site was unknown for countless years, combine to give the village its popularized name. Charcoal remains taken from a 20-foot, 4-inch pit at the village site have indicated — through carbon dating — that Indians lit campfires in the area over 2,400 years ago! Through excavation and long hours of research, considerably more than Indian artifacts and charcoal remains were found at the site. Among the surprises that were uncovered were the remains of an aged whaling cantina..., thought to have been in existence in the 1860s! Of interest at this point is the information that from 1861 to 1884 a lively, and quite profitable, whaling station was located at nearby Whaler's Cove (now a part of Point Lobos Reserve).

With the preceding information giving a brief indication as to the historic significance of the San Jose Creek area, it should also be added that it is in the same vicinity that the ghostly figure of a "long-ago-lady" has frequently been seen. Described in a variety of ways by angry and quite shaken Highway One motorists, the "mysterious matron of Monastery Beach" is most often observed crossing the road..., totally oblivious to cars screeching to a stop around her or violently swerving to avoid hitting her. Lost in her own spiritual world and forever hurrying on her way, the ghostly figure is soon lost to sight..., never leaving a trace of where she came from, where she is going, who she may be, or what never-ending mission she is so intent on carrying out...

A short walk from San Jose Creek brings one to Point Lobos Reserve. Described as "The Greatest Meeting of Land and Water in the World", this Punta de los Lobos Marinos (Point of the Sea Wolves) is blessed with one of the Big Sur coast's most interesting histories.

Aside from having been won in a game of chance, the colorful history of this area includes such things as shipwrecks, pirates, gold mines, smuggling, treasures, rum-running and, as previously indicated, a profitable and quite active whaling industry. Also included in the history of Point Lobos are a variety of strange and supernatural happenings. Among the strangest of the tales is the story of a prehistoric race that once inhabited the jagged headlands and rocky cliffs of this Pacific promontory. This belief was shared by those of the occult, and the tale was recorded long ago in an aged publication pertaining to happenings in and around the area of old Carmel. As the story goes, Point Lobos of the dim and distant past was "a veritable Garden of Eden", and was lived in by people of high intelligence who enjoyed lives of simplicity, security and tranquility.

All went well for this forgotten race until a serpent came to their Eden, bringing with it a black poison of selfishness and greed. It was this "poison" that brought ruin to the long-ago race (as has been the history of so many lost cultures). With this short and sad tale coming to an end, and for those who know Point Lobos well, it is of importance to add that the tale concludes with the information that the twisted and gnarled trees that are so much a part of the picturesqueness of the Point Lobos park, are but the reincarnation of souls of this lost race who are "doomed to haunt the shadowy places" until a race of god-like men return to the land.

Perhaps, with this concluding statement in mind, the age-old mystery of the origin of the warped and wind-sculptured Monterey cypress is solved. Perhaps these famed trees that cling so tenaciously to the rocks and headlands of Point Lobos, and to selected nearby promontories along the Monterey coast (and are found no place else in the world), are truly lost souls from a lost race..., entrapped with earthbound roots and waiting for a time that may never come...

Wind-sculptured and picturesque Point Lobos trees also play a part in the ghostly tale of a lost shipwreck treasure. As the story goes, long ago, when Monterey was the capital community of Alta California, a Spanish galleon fell victim to a fierce Pacific storm. Upon being dashed upon the rocks of Point Lobos, three survivors managed to reach the safety of shore..., each burdened with a portion of the ship's valuable cargo. Not knowing where they had landed and concerned as to what to do with their newly acquired wealth, the threesome decided to bury their loot and set out together in search of the nearest town.

Upon finding a warped and wind-blown Monterey cypress — amidst a miniature forest of like trees — they sighted through a crotch of the aged tree and planted the treasure where a gnarled limb pointed.

With the treasure hidden and all telltale traces carefully concealed, the tired trio began following a path, hoping it would lead them to civilization. To their delight they soon discovered they were not far from the bay-side town of Monterey. With light hearts and a shared secret they strode into the capital community and made their way to the nearest saloon. As one salute followed another, it was not long before one of the boastful three let the free-flowing whiskey get the best of him. With slurred tongue and bleary eyes he began to tell all who would listen of their good fortune! However, before he had a chance to tell the entire tale, his two companions jumped him and effectively put a silence to his boasts.

Unfortunately for the shipwreck survivors, the many Montereyans who made up the crowd at the saloon had had their appetites whetted by the tale..., and wanted to hear more about the treasure! In the ensuing events a fight broke out, resulting in the death of two of the sailors and the mysterious disappearance of the third. With no one left to reveal the hiding place, and after several treasure-seeking expeditions failed to find the aged cypress (with its gnarled limb "pointing the way"), the story was forgotten by all but a few.

Years later, during the days of whaling at Point Lobos, a lone Indian (who worked as a whaler at Whaler's Cove) told of finding the hidden shipwreck treasure. After having learned of the buried booty, and after having spent many months in a dedicated search, he told of finding a cypress that matched the description of the tree in the tale. After sighting through the crotch of the aged tree he saw the remains of a gnarled limb that pointed to the ground. Upon marking the tree he returned late that night with tools in hand. Carefully digging where the limb pointed, the blade of his shovel soon scraped against something metallic.

With visions of riches welling up in his mind, the Indian

dropped to his knees to inspect his find. However, just as his fingers groped for the valuables, a mysterious light appeared off the point and through the trees. Alarmed by the strange and unearthly glow, the frightened Indian took no chances and frantically began filling in the hole! With the treasure once again buried, and thinking that the ghosts of the shipwreck survivors were watching over their hidden hoard, or perhaps that the spirit of the long-dead ship captain was angry with him for trying to steal his cargo, the superstitious Indian left on the run..., vowing never to return to the treasure site, or tell anyone where he had found the ill-fated fortune...

The tale of a second shipwreck with a strange and ghostly twist also took place in the Point Lobos area. Although the wreck dates back to the late 1800s, the ghostly events surrounding it were not fully recorded for more than a quarter of a century. As the story unfolds, several seafarers from turn-of-the-century vessels reported hearing the subdued sounds of a submerged bell as they plied the Pacific off the Point Lobos promontory. Confused as to the sound, and wondering if it signalled the grave of a lost ship, speculation arose among coastal travelers as to the meaning of the bell-like sounds.

With time marching on, reports of the eerie sounds continued to haunt the men who sailed the treacherous waters of Point Lobos. Finally, the mysterious ringing of the underwater bell became too much for an aged and bewhiskered Pacific captain, and he hired a diver and crew to find its source.

Knowing the dangerous deep water dives that would ensue, as well as the slim chances of actually finding the bell, the San Francisco-based diver who accepted the job did so only at the insistence of the aged shipmaster..., and only then when the price was right. In following a chart supplied by the skipper (who had plotted the locations of where he had heard the bell's sounds, and who accompanied the men aboard the diving boat), the diver made repeated attempts to find the submerged source. Finally, on the second day of the search while resting at the bottom of the sea, the veteran diver heard a subdued and distant bell-like sound. Waiting in the underwater world of the Pacific he again heard "a vague wavering tone"..., almost as if a bell had been struck long before and the ringing sounds were slowly dying in the sea. In following the eerie submarine sounds he came to a ledge that appeared "to drop forever"..., and from which the ringing seemed to fill the sea!

After rising to the surface and reporting his find, as well as the danger that would be involved in making a dive into the darkened depths of the "bottomless canyon", the diver — at the urging of the captain — hesitatingly agreed to make one last dive..., in a final effort to find the bell and the ship from which it came.

Because of the depth of the submarine canyon, and because of his concern as to the many dangers involved, the diver gave detailed instructions to his crew. He also took special precautions in checking his heavy canvas diving suit and the cumbersome helmet that screwed to its top. Assured that all was right, and with the helmet carefully secured, he signaled that he was ready to begin, and pushed himself from the vessel's over-side ladder.

Being lowered ever so slowly, it seemed like forever before he reached the depths of the Point Lobos chasm. Finally, as his weighted shoes and groping hands touched a "shadowy something" near the canyon's bottom, a large seaweed-covered hulk began to emerge beside him. Reaching out in an effort to grasp something solid, the startled diver was surprised at the object's slippery feel, and realized immediately that he had been lowered directly on top of a lost ship!

Concerned as to the extreme depth of his dive and the terrific pressure that exerted itself on his suit, combined with the knowledge that he had completed his part of the bargain by finding the vessel from which the mysterious bell sounds came, the diver signalled his crew to bring him up. As he felt the tug of his life line, and started to clear the rotting remains of the aged hulk, he reached out for an object that he could take with him..., some tangible evidence that he had actually found a sunken ship. On clearing what he thought to be the upper works of the vessel, and where he was better able to view the ship's shadowy outline, he saw what appared to be a piece of wood jutting toward him at an awkward angle. Upon grasping the slippery, seaweed-covered object as he went by, it gave to his pull and rode to the surface with him.

After a long and purposely slow ascent, the diver was totally exhausted when he reached the launch and had to be dragged aboard the boat. As he lay on the deck, too tired to move, concerned crew members hastily unscrewed the helmet's face plate. With the face plate and helmet finally removed, and after having been revived by a fresh ocean breeze, the diver saw that the captain was anxiously studying the seaweed-covered board that he had brought to the surface. On examining the barnacle-encrusted and worm-eaten wood, the skipper realized that it was the remains of a ship's name-board.

Together the diver and captain carefully scraped the ocean growth from the rotting wood, and together they saw the name MAID OF ARDEN carved into the aged board. With the sudden realization of what the lost ship's name was, the captain became a changed man. His face took on a peculiar look and his voice shook with emotion as he announced to the crew that he was going to don the diving gear and visit the sunken vessel!

Neither the dangers involved, nor the emotional pleas of the veteran diver, would change the captain's mind. He had paid well for the trip, and it was he who was in sole command. With a suit fitted to the aged Pacific skipper, instructions were given and the dreaded dive began.

As the captain's helmet became lost in a flurry of foam and bubbles, the diving boat crew uneasily went about their duties, checking and rechecking the air hose and life line. Suddenly, almost as if it had been expected, the crew member in charge of the air hose frantically hollered for help as the furiously bubbling line came coiling to the surface unattached! Jumping for the life line, the men hurriedly pulled it to the surface..., only to realize that it, too, was unattached! A quick check of the lines revealed the reason — both lines had been cut by the captain!

As word spread up and down the coast of the strange circumstances surrounding the death of the aged shipmaster, the final chapter of the tale began to unfold. And, as perhaps would be expected, it was the nameboard of the sunken vessel that proved to be the key that unlocked the mystery. Upon learning the name of the wrecked ship, a veteran Pacific seafarer (who had known the lost captain) offered the information that the MAID OF ARDEN had long ago set out from San Francisco on a voyage down the California coast..., never to be heard from again! With this information adding to the story, the seafarer's next statement answered, for many, the question of why the lonely captain chose to die among the bones of this ship. Aboard the MAID OF ARDEN on that fateful last voyage was the skipper's wife, a lady whose spirit he perhaps had been seeking, and a spirit that may have beckoned to him through the sounds of a bell..., summoning him to her side and to the Point Lobos deep where she had long ago died...

Back on land, and in wandering the southerly trails of beautiful Point Lobos, one will come upon a picturesque inlet known as China Cove. This tiny inlet with its secluded sandy beach boasts a colorful history with stories of lost treasures, hidden caves, and long-ago smuggling connected with it. Among the most believable of the tales, and a story that is accepted by many as the basis for the origin of the cove's name, is an aged tale of Chinese smuggling. As the story goes, approximately one century ago, soon after the introduction of the Chinese Exclusion Bill (1882), the business of smuggling Chinese into California became a profitable pastime. Among the landings favored for this purpose by one enterprising ship captain was the secluded inlet now known as China Cove.

With this brief background serving as an introduction to our next tale (a tale that is also "touched on" in the author's book "GHOSTS, BANDITS AND LEGENDS of old Monterey"), it is important to mention that slightly to the south of Point Lobos Reserve is the cliff-clinging community of Carmel Highlands. Among the most captivating of all California's coastal villages, Carmel Highlands, with its dense Pacific fogs, cliff-side homes, and narrow, twisting, tree-lined streets..., lends itself to ghostly tales as few communities do.

Among the best known of the tales, and a tale that is thought to be directly linked to the colorful history of China Cove, is the story of several dozen Chinese workers who were buried alive in a Highlands coal mine. With its corporation papers dating back to the 1880s (and soon after the business of smuggling Chinese went into high gear), the Carmelo Land & Coal Company "officially" began operation. Although home-based in the area of Carmel Highlands, the coal (which is reported to have been of highly gaseous content) was drawn from a lengthy tunnel and 275-foot shaft located to the east of the cliff-clinging community.

All went well for members of the coal company during its initial years of operation; however, as time went on, several problems arose. Among the problems were a bunker fire and ship explosion at their Whaler's Cove loading facility (of nearby Point Lobos). These, and other problems that plagued the company, resulted in financial difficulties for the mine's backers. With a payroll to meet — and little money in the till — it is rumored that the mine operators herded their workers into the lengthy tunnel and blasted it shut! This simple act (regardless of how inhuman it may have been) conveniently solved the company's payroll problem and did away with the troublesome mine in one operation.

The question of whether or not there were between 40 and 70 Chinese workers lost at the Highlands mine (as has been reported in other publications) has been debated by historians of the Monterey Peninsula-Big Sur areas for many years. A similar story that persists to this day states that there definitely was a cave-in burying many of the mine's Chinese laborers..., but it wasn't financial problems that were to blame for the gruesome event. This story goes on to tell of a deadly and highly contagious disease (either smallpox or a type of plague, depending on which tale one wishes to believe) that was being carried by a limited number of the mine's workers. Rather than taking a chance on letting the disease spread, subscribers to this theory believe that the entire crew of Chinese laborers was sent down the lengthy shaft..., as the mine's only entrance (and exit) was forever sealed. Finally, before leaving this subject for an additional Highlands tale, a second mention of the Carmelo Land & Coal Company's financial problems is perhaps in order. When discussing the many rumors that circulate about the mine with an aged member of a pioneer south coast family (now deceased), he matter-of-factly stated that even though the Chinese laborers worked the mine "from dawn till dusk for ten cents a day", the owners of the mine were losing money, and rather than attempt to pay their help or let them go..., they chose to entomb the workers within the mine's deep shaft.

Today, with no records of who or how many Chinese were smuggled into China Cove (not to mention other inlets along the California coast), and no way of knowing whether or not there actually were a number of Chinese buried alive in the Carmel Highlands mine (without uncovering the lengthy shaft), one can only shake his head in wonder as he stands in the area of the old mine, marveling at the rusted relics of yesterday and listening to the eerie sounds of the wind as it blows up the canyons and plays in the trees..., sounding for all the world like mournful cries emitting from some hidden hollow deep within the Highlands hillside...

Other than the spirits of several dead Chinese that may linger in the area of the long-closed Carmel

Highlands coal mine, there are a number of haunted hillside houses that add to the mystique of this cliff-clinging community. One of these buildings is an elaborate multi-storied structure that is perched high on a Highlands hill overlooking the Pacific.

Dark, foreboding, and scary to look at, this 50-plus-year-old building has been empty for a considerable period of time and is thought by some to be a refuge for troubled spirits. It is these reasons, plus the knowledge that the dwelling's original owner (and builder) was a rather unique lady who believed in such things as spiritualism and the teachings of Amie Semple McPherson, that has prompted people to speculate as to the possibility of the mysterious goings on being the work of "visitors from the other side" who have returned to the house to honor some special occasion..., just as they did when the owner was alive.

Among the ghostly occurrences that have been attributed to this structure, and which have been experienced by numerous people, are such things as doors that mysteriously open and close, lights that turn on and off, and heavy footsteps that are sometimes heard. A bit more unusual in the way of the supernatural, and a happening that may be connected with the sounds of heavy footsteps, are loud thumping noises that have been traced to the building's third story. Because they appear to come from a bedroom, and because they are described as similar to sounds that heavy shoes would make if they were dropped on a floor, more than one visitor has been led to believe that a long-ago guest had returned to a familiar room and thoughtfully (and noisily) removed his shoes before stretching out on the bed for a well-deserved rest.

Although the building's spooky appearance and unexplained happenings are difficult to dismiss from one's mind, the most unnerving of the structure's many experiences are intense feelings of "not being wanted" that, at times, seem to fill the house. Because these feelings (or vibrations, as they have often been described) have frequently been experienced, several past inhabitants are of the opinion that the dwelling's

The Carmelite Monastery as it appeared approximately one-half century ago. It is San Jose Creek, upon whose banks this imposing edifice was built, that the author has chosen as the Big Sur coast's northerly starting point. It is also near this structure that the ghostly figure of the "mysterious matron of Monastery Beach" has frequently been seen. L. Josselyn photo, P. Hathaway Collection.

Point Lobos Reserve boasts one of the Big Sur coast's most colorful histories. Shown above is one of its picturesque promontories, with the secluded entrance of Whaler's Cove seen to the left. Inset shows the Veteran Cypress, a gnarled and aged Point Lobos tree. As indicated in the text, perhaps the earthbound roots of this tree contain the troubled souls of a forgotten race. P. Hathaway Collection photos.

Situated near the mouth of Palo Colorado Canyon was the coastal community of Notley's Landing. Among other distinctions, this long-gone settlement boasted the "wildest dance hall" along the Monterey County coast. Bancroft Library Collection. Inset shows the precarious positioning of this vanished village. H. Lyons photo, P. Hathaway Collection.

Almost hidden by the foliage of Palo Colorado Canyon are the ghostly remains of long-ago lumber mills. A close look at this neglected equipment brings to mind a time that was. R.A. Reinstedt photos & Collection.

The Monterey Lime Company played an important part in the history of Bixby Canyon during the early years of this century. About all that is left of this colorful period are the kilns' ghostly chimneys that still point toward the heavens. Inset shows a portion of the aerial tramway that transported buckets of lime down the rugged canyon. P. Hathaway Collection photos.

Situated on the very edge of Bixby Point were Monterey Lime Company buildings and the end of the line for the aerial tramway. L. Josselyn photo, P. Hathaway Collection. Also on the cliffs of Bixby Point was a somewhat rickety-appearing chute (inset), where barrels of lime were loaded aboard small coastal freighters. California State Library Collection.

The building of the coast road was a magnificent feat, with the construction of Bixby Creek Bridge considered by many to have been the crowning achievement of the entire project. Although there are many tales that circulate about the bridge and the rugged canyon that it crosses, perhaps the most talked about of the tales is the account of a ghostly airplane of World War One vintage that flies under the bridge's gracefully curving arch (shown — soon after construction — in the inset photo). Of continued interest to this tale is the fact that people still speak of hearing the sounds of an airplane as it flies under the arch and up the narrow canyon. L. Josselyn photo, P. Hathaway Collection photos.

As indicated in the text, ghosts mean different things to different people, and ghosts are thought to come in a variety of shapes and sizes. It is with this in mind that the story of the MACON is included. Truly an incredible aircraft, the loss of this giant dirigible was also an incredible loss to the United States and to "lighter-than-air" buffs throughout the world. Being 785 feet long, and containing five Curtiss Sparrowhawk fighter-scout planes in her hull, the magnificent MACON was a victim of circumstances and fell to a watery death off the Big Sur coast on February 12, 1935. National Archives Collection #80-CF-4163-15. Inset shows the 3,000-ton coastal freighter BABINDA before her final fire-ravaged voyage down the Big Sur coast. M. Plapp Collection.

The Point Sur rock and lighthouse are familiar landmarks to both travelers of Highway One and seafarers of the Big Sur coast. Claiming numerous vessels over the years, the waters of this Pacific graveyard contain the remains of the MACON and the BABINDA, as well as the "twin" shipwrecks of the VENTURA and LOS ANGELES. Inset shows two of the structures that are perched atop this famed Point Sur promontory. P. Hathaway Collection photos.

Considered a sacred mountain by certain Indians of the Monterey County coast, Pico Blanco (White Mountain or Peak) may also hold the secret to Big Sur's mysterious "lost world". L. Josselyn photo, P. Hathaway Collection.

The cabin of Alfred K. Clark (Uncle Al) as it appeared in the early 1930s. It was near this cabin that Clark (inset) discovered the Silver King Mine and Big Sur's subterranean world of "elephants with long shaggy hair" and "cats with long sharp teeth". R. Woicekowski Collection photos.

This one hundred-plus-year-old-house still sits near the top of a ridge just south of the Big Sur park. It was this dwelling that at one time marked the end of the line for people who were traveling south on the old coast road. A look at the history of this Big Sur landmark also indicates that it once boasted a post office..., as well as a ghost! L. Josselyn photo, P. Hathaway Collection.

Long before man scarred the landscape with dynamite and dump trucks, the Big Sur coast was a primitive and peaceful paradise. Perhaps it was during these long-ago years that the Santa Lucia's mysterious dark watchers surveyed the scene with satisfaction and content..., rather than with modern-day fears of people and pollution. L. Josselyn photo, P. Hathaway Collection.

One of the many mysteries of the Los Burros Mining District area are the century old bones that were yielded by Massacre Cave. J.L. Crisan Jr. photo & Collection.

A true ghost of the past is the mining community of Manchester. Known to many as "The Lost City of the Santa Lucias", this mountain town of yesterday was the hub of Monterey County's remote Los Burros Mining District, and its site is not far from the mysterious Ghost of Gold claim. M. Fisher photo, Monterey Savings & Loan Collection.

The Gem Saloon was among the favorite gathering places for the people of the mining community of Manchester. Monterey County Library Collection.

Willie Cruikshank, founder of the Los Burros Mining District's best paying mine. Willie's disappearance adds to the many mysteries of Monterey's mother lode. Adrian Harbolt Collection.

original owner still claims the aged residence as her own..., and, even though she is no longer among the living, she is letting it be known that she still craves the privacy she sought when alive. In carrying this thought one step further..., it is of interest to note that when the structure was being built, the lady of the house had a secret passageway installed within the dwelling..., a passageway that enabled her to "disappear at will" and maintain the privacy she so avidly sought...

While on the subject of spiritualism, old houses, and ladies connected with them, one cannot help but think of Sarah Winchester and the famed Winchester Mystery House of San Jose, California. Guided by her spirit friends, and built as they directed, the 160-room Winchester mansion is perhaps the world's best example of what unlimited funds and a belief in the occult can lead to. According to tradition, and documented in several sources, the widowed Mrs. Winchester was told by a Massachusetts medium that she could gain eternal life, as well as escape the angry spirits of those killed by the Winchester rifle, if she were to acquire, and continually add to, a west coast dwelling. With this being her goal, the diminutive Sarah Winchester traveled to the San Jose area and purchased an existing farmhouse. With this eight-room house as the beginning, Sarah spent the next 38 years of her life in creating the bizarre, but beautiful, Winchester mansion.

Although it is believed that the closest Sarah Winchester ever got to Carmel Highlands was Monterey's magnificent Hotel Del Monte, there are those who feel her influence did reach the picturesque coastal community. Evidence of this is an elaborate hillside house that boasts a history of constantly being added to. Even though it is not nearly as large as the Winchester edifice, nevertheless local legend states that the lady of the house was under the impression that as long as she kept building... she would never die. Among the results of this building spree is a lavish multi-roomed mansion boasting, among other things, seven bedrooms..., all elegantly appointed and all with fireplaces (the largest being big enough for a man to walk into).

Without going into more detail about this haunted hillside house (as the author previously documented this account in his book "GHOSTLY TALES AND MYSTERIOUS HAPPENINGS of old Monterey"), it should be mentioned — for the benefit of ghost enthusiasts — that the elaborate structure includes a detached library building where several odd occurrences have been reported. Among these occurrences, and taking place behind locked doors, are the sounds of the building's original owner as she pleads with the butler to let her leave...

In moving from Carmel Highlands to locations farther south, one crosses Mal Paso Creek (meaning bad crossing) where long-ago travelers experienced many trying times. It is also near this spot, more than a half-century ago, that a wagon driver lost his life to the rugged terrain. For many years after the driver fell to his death down a Santa Lucia cliff, people who traveled the aged trail at night spoke of hearing sounds resembling the bells from the collar of the team's lead horse. As if this isn't enough to make one pause and wonder..., it is of interest to add that the bell sounds were the loudest at the exact spot where the team, the wagonload of tanbark (used for the tanning of hides), and the frantic driver fell from the road to the canyon below...

In continuing on our journey toward the heart of Big Sur, we pass canyons and coves where tales of long-ago pirates, lost treasures, mysterious church bells, and an invisible wagon and its equally invisible team, add to the interest of this coastal wilderness. Among these canyons, and home to the clatter and confusion of the ghostly wagon and its spirited steeds (discussed in the author's book "GHOSTLY TALES AND MYSTERIOUS HAPPENINGS of old Monterey"), is the history-rich area of Palo Colorado Canyon (meaning redwood, red stick, red mast, etc.).

Situated near the mouth of this Santa Lucia canyon was a seaside village that was considered the most active settlement of its kind along the Big Sur coast. Even though most historians know Notley's Landing as a shipping point for timber (including shakes, shingles, posts, railroad ties and tanbark), the small coastal community has also been noted as a haven for smugglers (of the Chinese and illegal liquor variety), as well as for containing the "wildest dance hall" along the lengthy Monterey County coast.

Other than its colorful history of wild dance halls, long-ago smuggling, shipping of timber, and invisible wagons, the area around Palo Colorado Canyon is also known for such things as a ghostly ship nestled high on a hillside (and completely hidden by trees and foliage), hard-to-get-to waterfalls, beautiful scenery (boasting more native California trees than any area of comparable size in the state), abandoned lumber mills (and their cumbersome equipment), towering redwoods, lost silver mines..., and the ghostly figure of a pretty young lass that, in days of old, was frequently seen along the swiftly flowing Palo Colorado creek.

In attempting to track down the story behind the ghostly image of this south coast maiden, two aged members of a respected Monterey Peninsula family shared with the author the following short tale. Many years ago, perhaps even prior to the turn of the century, an attractive young lady who lived in the canyon lost her life to a sad set of circumstances. It was not long after her death that residents of the canyon reported seeing her image — during moonlit nights — on the banks of the Santa Lucia stream. Seen by numerous people over a period of many years, the long-ago young lady appeared quite happy and was always observed busily combing her hair. As to why she was preoccupied with her hair, the old-timers did not know; however, there seemed to be complete agreement in the thought that if it kept her happy and eased her pain..., it was a fine way to remember Palo Colorado Canyon's pretty young miss with the long golden hair...

Down the road and around a few bends, one comes upon Bixby Canyon and the magnificent Bixby Creek Bridge. Beautiful to look at, and considered the "engineering triumph" of the coast road, the Bixby Bridge (originally known as Rainbow Bridge and described as one of the world's highest and longest single-span arch bridges) draws visitors from far and near who marvel at its construction and gaze from its vistas. (An interesting sidelight notes that it was from a Bixby Bridge vista in 1938 that a herd of sea otters was spotted. This sighting was of major importance as sea otters had not been seen for many years and were thought to have been extinct.)

Even though the Bixby Creek Bridge was completed nearly a half century ago (dedicated in November of 1932), and for many local residents has "always been" one of the highlights of the Big Sur coast..., this was not always the case. Long before the Bixby Bridge was even a dream, the Monterey Lime Company (of Bixby Canyon) also drew visitors from far and near to view an aerial tramway that transported enormous buckets of lime down the rugged canyon to distant Bixby Point (where it was loaded aboard small coastal freighters). Unfortunately, this turn-of-the-century industry — as had a lumber industry many years before — did not survive for long, and soon became little more than a memory. Among the modern-day "ghosts" of this bygone era are huge chimneys from aged lime kilns that rise from a forest of poison oak and Santa Lucia chaparral. Reaching for the skies of the Big Sur coast, these gaunt survivors of yesteryear remind passersby of a long-ago time when Bixby Canyon was alive with people..., rather than forgotten ghosts of the past.

Ghostly tales of a different nature connected with the Bixby Creek Canyon can perhaps be attributed to a construction worker who is said to have fallen into the concrete pour during the building of the bridge's north column..., or to one (or more) of the five restaurant workers who lost their lives during a 1948 "massacre" along the canyon's rim.

On not so grisly a note, perhaps the Bixby tale that tops them all is the story of a ghostly airplane of World War One vintage that has been observed approaching the south coast canyon from the Pacific. As if seeing the ghostly image of an aged double-wing airplane "zeroing in" on Bixby Bridge isn't enough to unnerve one on its own, the fact that the pilot of this frail craft flies straight up the canyon — and under the arch of the bridge — makes those who are aware of the story (and who, to this day, claim to hear sounds of the airplane echoing off the canyon walls) wonder who the "spirited" pilot is..., and why he repeatedly risks his life — as well as his craft — in this daring display of Bixby boldness...

While on the subject of strange aircraft of the Big Sur coast, the author feels the following tale, even though it strays a bit from the subject of ghosts, should be included in a work of this type.

Said to have occurred in the 1950s, the tale (although not common knowledge at the time, and not related to the author until several years, and perhaps versions, later) is described as having created quite a stir among those who were aware of it. According to people in the know, the "happening" took place on a dark south coast night when a teen-age couple was parked along a narrow and lonely country road. The road, which was private, unpaved and seldom used, led off the Big Sur Highway and toward the heart of the Santa Lucias. After having found a suitable place to stop, and after having been parked for a period of time, the darkness of the night and the peacefulness of the scene was suddenly shattered by an incredibly bright light! Staring in shocked silence at the light, the teen-agers told of seeing a huge circular-shaped object that hovered over the area they had recently driven. Terrified at what they saw, and being only a few hundred yards from the light source, the couple watched in wide-eyed wonder as the low flying craft's unearthly light lit up the landscape as if it were day!

After the initial shock of seeing the strange object began to lessen, the boy (who was a photography student at a local high school, and who faithfully carried his equipment with him) grabbed his camera and, with extreme caution, he and his partner crept from their car. With a hush in the air and not a breath of wind stirring, the teen-agers took pains not to break the unnatural silence. As the enormous circular-shaped object and its brilliant "crown of light" continued to hover, the young lad took several pictures of the strange craft.

Suddenly, completely without warning, and at a pace faster than the eye could follow, the mystery craft "shot" to a spot directly above the shaken couple! Bathed in the glow of a halo-like luminescence, the teen-agers clung to each other and shielded their eyes from the blinding light. Too scared to cry, and knowing it was useless to run, the couple huddled together and awaited their fate. Finally, after what seemed like an eternity, the huge craft and its eerie light disappeared from sight as quickly and quietly as it had originally appeared. Ecstatic with joy and not waiting for an encore, the thankful couple jumped into their car and raced from the scene!

The following day the boy took his camera to school and, in the privacy of the high school's darkroom, he developed the film. Elated at the quality of his pictures and the brilliance with which the mysterious ring appeared, he proudly showed the film to his instructor. Amazed and concerned as to what the object was, the photography teacher wasted little time in notifying authorities. With amazing rapidity the film was confiscated..., never to be seen again by the boy or his instructor.

At this writing it is unknown where the film is, what type of craft (or illusion) made the strange light, or what became of the young photographer. What is known (or at least what is still talked about by those in the know), is that a second, and perhaps interrelated, mystery exists to this day as to what it was that caused a huge circular imprint on the grass of a large clearing — not far from where the couple spotted the ringed aircraft! Discovered not long after the sighting had taken place, the account of the circular-shaped marking (which was described as "huge in nature" and "having left a burned imprint on the grass") adds considerable interest to the story of Big Sur's mystery craft, and makes one wonder what type of object it was that touched down in the Santa Lucia wilderness..., and what — if any — strange creatures may have exited from its hold.

Before one totally discounts this tale as a wild dream of UFO (Unidentified Flying Object) enthusiasts, it is of interest to note that over the years several mysterious objects have been reported in the vicinity of the Big Sur coast. The brief account that follows — from a 1950 issue of the Monterey Peninsula Herald — serves as proof to non-believers that documentation of such sightings does exist. Included in the report is the information that a Monterey woman saw "a brilliantly lighted object... streaking over the ocean... off Carmel Highlands". While this report is interesting on its own, a second account (from the same source), contains information that is more in keeping with the preceding tale. According to the newspaper article, a lady from the nearby community of Chualar (on the east side of the Santa Lucia Mountains), told of an object that "swooped down" over her car, giving off "a strange bluish-white light that hurt our eyes like a welder's torch". With this account fitting in nicely with the previously-told teen-ager's tale (and with more than one person having been in the car to witness the event), one begins to wonder if what she saw, and what the young Monterey Peninsula couple saw, could have been the same unidentified object..., an object that, over a quarter of a century ago, visited the mountains of the Santa Lucias and left its calling card in the form of a singed ring of grass...

With the interesting story of strange, and possibly outer space, aircraft having touched down on a coastal mountain flat, one can't help but think about the often-told tales of the Santa Lucia's mysterious "dark watchers". Frequently discussed by historians and pioneer settlers of the Big Sur coast, the existence of such creatures — whether they be human or from some far-distant planet — has created considerable controversy among many of the area's aged residents for many years.

The fact that the "watchers" have been described by two of Monterey County's literary greats, both of whom knew the coastal mountains well, adds a certain credence to the stories, and has helped make the question as to the identity of the "human-like" forms one of the area's most puzzling mysteries.

John Steinbeck, born in the nearby community of Salinas, and winner of the Nobel and Pulitzer Prizes for literature, told of the dark watchers in his short story "Flight", describing them as "a dark form against the sky, a man's figure standing on top of a rock". Robinson Jeffers, a long-time Monterey Peninsula resident and world-known for his poetry, described the mysterious figures in his poem "Such Counsels You Gave To Me", as "forms that look human... but certainly are not human". With these descriptions, both having been published in the 1930s, focusing attention on the Big Sur country's mysterious dark watchers, the existence of said creatures became internationally known. As would be expected, with the fame of these authors spreading worldwide, people from far and near came to see..., and people to this day keep a sharp eye open for the silent figures of the Santa Lucias. (The preceding dark watcher descriptions by Steinbeck and Jeffers are admittedly brief, requiring one to read the complete texts for further meaning and content.)

With a short section of his book "GHOSTLY TALES AND MYSTERIOUS HAPPENINGS of old Monterey", devoted to the dark watchers (and a sighting made by a prominent Monterey Peninsula resident in the mid-1960s), the author is reluctant to repeat the tale here. However, after learning of the possible "touchdown" of a space craft in the Santa Lucias, and after pondering the possibility of such a happening, he finds it interesting to speculate as to how many such craft (if any) may have touched down in this coastal wilderness during centuries past. Also, if in fact there actually was a singed ring of grass left as a "calling card" by a mysterious space vehicle, the author wonders if it was the first (and only) such "memento" to have been left in the mountains of Big Sur. In following this thought one step further, it is of interest to note that old-timers state there are places — deep within the heart of the Santa Lucias — that have never been fully explored (except, of course, by Indians of a past age). This thought makes one wonder all the more if such "unexplored places" harbor the sites of other visitations and forgotten mementos.

With these thoughts in mind, and with the thoughts of mysterious dark watchers, strange circular-shaped aircraft, singed rings of grass, and unexplored wilderness areas, all a part of the "storied" history of Big Sur (combined with the fact that much of the above-listed information has come from a variety of unrelated sources), one can't help but carry these thoughts one step further and wonder if — perchance — the mysterious dark watchers could be beings from a far-off planet..., beings that may have originally visited this area at some long-ago time, and beings who, to this day, may roam the mountains and valleys of the Santa Lucias guarding mysterious secrets of their own...

Ghosts mean different things to different people. It is with this statement in mind that the author feels ghosts must also come in a variety of shapes, sizes and forms. The following tale, as have the past three, strays a bit from the norm (as far as "traditional" ghost stories are concerned) and once again involves a visitor from the sky..., a visitor that has become a unique, intriguing, and factual part of the fascinating history of Big Sur. Taking place south of Bixby Canyon, and south of the lonely mountain road from which the teen-age couple spotted the mysterious luminous craft..., the story instead takes place off the Big Sur coast and in the vicinity of the massive rock promontory known as Point Sur.

Occurring on February 12, 1935, the account tells of the loss of Uncle Sam's magnificent MACON..., the last of America's super dirigibles. This aircraft was so large that if she were to have been placed on end, her nose would have reached higher than a 75-story skyscraper! Having been lost due to a combination of problems (including turbulent air and a weakened top tail fin), this "dinosaur of the skies" — complete with five double-winged Curtiss Sparrowhawk fighter-scout planes that she carried in her hull — rests to this day in the waters off the Big Sur coast..., a truly incredible ghost of the past..., and a ghost that measures 785 feet in length!

Other ghosts, of the nautical type, that rest beneath the waters of Point Sur are discussed in the author's book "SHIPWRECKS AND SEA MONSTERS of California's Central Coast" (including a much more detailed account of the wreck of the MACON). Among these mishaps were the wrecks of the coastal steamers VENTURA (lost April 20, 1875) and LOS ANGELES (lost April 21, 1894). In borrowing a few lines from the above-mentioned book, the reader will soon discover why these mishaps are termed "twin" shipwrecks. "Both vessels were 'retired' government ships, both had been renovated for passenger service, both were owned by the Pacific Coast Steamship Company, both mishaps were due to negligence on the part of the ships' officers, both shipwrecks occurred in the vicinity of Point Sur, and both accidents took place in the month of April, within a day of each other, at approximately the same time of night — nineteen years apart!"

Of additional interest to Big Sur buffs, is the information that the survivors of both mishaps were cared for by people of the coast..., and the "spoils" of the wrecks (in the form of furnishings, linens, draperies, wool, 150 calves, and a large assortment of various foodstuffs), were put to good use by the people of the Sur. Also washed ashore (from the VENTURA) was a number of "knockdown wagons" which were quickly assembled by pioneer residents and were used throughout Big Sur for over three-quarters of a century. Of interest to readers who yearn for more in the way of ghosts is the information that there are those who still speak of hearing the "supernatural" sounds of the VENTURA's knockdown wagons as they hike the back trails of the Monterey County coast.

Perhaps the strangest, and certainly the most ghostly of the many shipwrecks of the Point Sur area, is the story of the 3,000-ton coastal freighter BABINDA which caught fire off Monterey Bay's north shore. The men of this aged all-wood vessel fought the flames until it became obvious to all aboard that they were fighting a losing battle. Abandoning their ship, thinking it was not long for this world, the crew of the freighter was picked up by the steamer CELILO and transported to the port of San Francisco.

Far from dead, the BABINDA seemed to take on a new life after her crew departed and, almost as if she had a mind of her own, she began her last — and certainly her most dramatic — voyage. Commanded by a phantom skipper, and guided by a ghostly crew, the BABINDA — with clouds of smoke billowing from her hold — drifted past the populous Monterey Peninsula (causing considerable concern as she went), past the treacherous Point Lobos promontory, and down the rugged Big Sur coast. Finally, with her ghost crew and captain arriving at their destination (more than a day after the ship had been abandoned), the burning BABINDA slipped beneath the waves of Point Sur at 7:10 A.M. on the fourth day of March, 1923.

In being frequently discussed by those interested in shipwrecks, as well as by ghost enthusiasts of the nautical type, the consensus seems to be that the phantom skipper knew exactly where he was going as he guided his crippled craft down California's central coast (a distance of approximately 40 miles)..., permitting her to die a dignified death amid the bones of several other lost ships..., in an area known to navigators and shipmasters alike as one of the west's most dreaded "Pacific graveyards"...

While in the vicinity of Point Sur, a brief account of Big Sur's mysterious "lost world" should be included. Even though the story is known to mining buffs of Monterey County through their research into Al Clark's Silver King Mine (and is discussed in detail in the author's book "TALES, TREASURES AND PIRATES of old Monterey"), it is a tale that borders on the incredible, and certainly befits the title of this work.

In touching briefly on the story's background, one should be aware that Alfred K. Clark, the man behind the tale, was told of the existence of a Santa Lucia silver mine by a dying Indian he had befriended. Upon learning that Spanish soldiers from their capital city quarters of Monterey had obtained "wire-silver" from Indians of the Little Sur area, it didn't take Clark long to realize that the mine was on (or near) land that he had homesteaded. (For those unfamiliar with Big Sur, the Little Sur section of the Monterey coast is slightly to the north of Point Sur and gains its name from the Little Sur River that flows through it.)

With the knowledge that a mine of considerable wealth might be on his property, the popular Al Clark (a Civil War veteran and known for his banjo playing as well as his eccentricities) wasted little time in seeking the mine's source. It was this search, and what he eventually discovered, that consumed the remaining years of this man's life. It was also this search and its discovery that turned Clark into a recluse..., and a living legend of the Sur.

Not divulging his secret until he was on his death bed, and only then to his most trusted friends, a delirious Al Clark told of breaking into a huge natural cavern while working to extend the mine's tunnel. Upon exploration of the immense underground opening, Clark discovered a second and third chamber..., as well as a subterranean river, albino fish, icicle- and cone-like rock formations, sparkling walls, Indian-like mortars, and ghostly likenesses of "elephants with long shaggy hair" and "cats with long sharp teeth".

Though his discoveries sounded a bit far-fetched, even to

those who were at the old man's side, upon looking at them with a critical eye, they (in most cases) proved to have plausible scientific explanations. The chambers, or underground caverns (whichever term may best apply), were, quite possibly, natural formations of limestone..., a type of rock that lends itself to such things, and a type of rock that is found in abundance in certain sections of the Little Sur. As a matter of record, Pico Blanco (White Peak or Mountain), located near the Silver King site, contains the highest quality of dolomite limestone of the entire central California coast. Limestone also lends itself to icicle- as well as cone-like formations (commonly referred to as stalactites and stalagmites) which are formed from the evaporation of dripping mineralized water (often found where there is a high concentration of lime). Subterranean rivers are also known to exist in limestone formations and, to make things of even more interest, the south fork of the Little Sur River is reported to flow underground in the area of the Silver King Mine. As to albino fish, creatures of this sort are sometimes found in underground rivers and are called troglobites (fish that lose their eyesight and body pigment due to the length of time they have lived in darkness). The sparkling walls that Clark referred to could have been the natural cave or cavern walls that contained flakes from a variety of reflective minerals. The mortars, to most people, meant that at some time long ago there was a natural entrance to this underground world (which may still exist), and that people of a past age worked and/or lived in the vast chambers.

Certainly of most interest, and without a doubt the most important of Uncle Al's discoveries, were the wall paintings of strange elephant- and cat-like creatures. These paintings were obviously meant to depict the mammoth or mastadon and the saber-toothed tiger. Creatures such as these are known to have roamed the California wilderness long before man was thought to be here. However, because their likenesses were depicted by man..., one begins to wonder just who the ghostly race of prehistoric people were who lived along the Big Sur coast, frequented a huge underground cavern, and painted pictures of creatures they saw..., creatures that existed thousands of years ago...

(Those who don't wish to let this fascinating story die, and who wish to speculate further as to its meaning..., may be interested in knowing that according to the mythology and beliefs of certain Indians of the Monterey County coast, the Little Sur's magnificent Pico Blanco was considered a sacred mountain..., a mountain where man had his beginning!)

In moving from the areas of Pico Blanco and the Little Sur, we pass through the beautiful Big Sur valley and come to a house high on a ridge and slightly to the south of the popular (Pfeiffer) Big Sur State Park. Today the house sits along busy Highway One, but at one time it marked the "end of the line" for travelers who were south-county bound on the old coast road (those who continued in a southerly direction did so by trail). This Big Sur landmark of over 100 years also served as a post office and gathering place for coastal residents..., and to this day is pointed out by old-timers as a Big Sur building with a ghostly past.

Although the ghost did not linger for long, it made the inhabitants of the house very much aware of it while it was there. In piecing the story together we find the ghost to have been that of a young Mexican lad who worked as a ranch hand and who shared a back room at the ridge house. One day while riding a horse in a nearby canyon, the boy was thrown from his mount and killed. After lamenting the loss of the likable lad, the occupants of the house began hearing familiar — and very discomforting — "middle-of-the-night" sounds..., sounds such as the boy's footsteps on the back porch and rapping (knocking) noises on the back door and windows.

Not about to open the door, the terrified inhabitants of the house frantically searched the building in hopes of finding something that the departed lad had returned to claim. Upon finding three "store-bought" collars that had belonged to the boy, residents of the ridge house quickly threw them out! From that moment on they were never again troubled by the ghost's frightening footsteps..., or by store-bought collars that belonged to the dead...

Also in the heart of the Big Sur country, and a landmark of more recent vintage, is a wayside inn that is to many the epitome of Big Sur and all things good. Nestled in a canyon, and blending with the redwoods and a brisk mountain stream, this rustic coastal haven had its beginning about the time Highway One was completed, and today looks back on nearly a half-century of memories. Among these memories are the times shared with the man who created this coastal retreat..., a man who, unfortunately, is no longer living. However, even though the original owner and builder of this "spot time forgot" no longer holds court at the long table within the inn, time after time both visitors and workers who have become a part of this Big Sur experience have reported feeling and seeing the presence of this unique individual. Dressed in familiar attire (complete with suspenders), this grand old man has appeared to those he knew, and has added feelings of warmth and good will to the list of experiences shared by a select group of guests who have had the good fortune of discovering the inn..., and who have stayed the night in "Papa's room".

One incident — which was not of the positive variety — that was experienced in Papa's special place occurred in the late 1970s. Even though it is the only happening of its type that has been recorded, it may be of interest to readers because of the innkeeper's concerns..., even before the incident took place. As reported to the author, early one afternoon, while raking leaves near Papa's room, the innkeeper noticed a rather young couple as they were escorted to the rustic, cabin-like quarters. Upon seeing the couple, the perceptive innkeeper (who had been one of Papa's most trusted friends and helpers) had doubts as to whether they were "right for the room". With the couple appearing happy and proceeding to move their luggage in, the hard working innkeeper decided to let the matter rest, and continued with his raking and his afternoon chores.

As evening came and the inn's restaurant became a gathering place for guests and good friends, the innkeeper put his concerns aside and acted as host to those who partook of the excellent food, the classical music, and the warmth of the building's many fireplaces. Along about 9:30, as the evening began to mellow, the phone suddenly rang..., spoiling the atmosphere and the coziness of the scene. Upon answering the call, the innkeeper's original doubts came back to haunt him..., as on the other end of the line was the man who had registered to stay in Papa's room. Calling from a second Big Sur location, the troubled man indicated that he and his wife had left "in a hurry" and that they wouldn't be spending the night. In continuing, the man said that in their haste to get out of the room they had left some of their belongings for which they would return in the morning.

Considerably concerned, and wondering what had taken place, the innkeeper immediately crossed the yard to check the room and make sure all was in order. Upon reaching the cabin that had so recently been vacated, he was surprised — and annoyed — to find the door wide open and the couple's things scattered about. On entering the room to turn the lights out, the innkeeper immediately sensed his departed friend's presence. Not only was Papa's presence stronger than he had ever felt it before, but the innkeeper also sensed that Papa wished to be left ALONE! With the message quite clear, the innkeeper excused himself, bade Papa good night, and quietly and quickly turned off the light and closed the door.

Early the next morning the couple returned for their belongings, not mentioning what had taken place the night before, and not asking for their money back. To this day the innkeeper has difficulty explaining what it was about the couple that made him feel they were not right for the room, and he doesn't know what they experienced on the night in question. However, he does take satisfaction in knowing that whatever it was that made him feel the way he did..., it was shared by Papa in no uncertain terms!

With all other experiences of a supernatural nature being of the positive variety..., and with Papa "posthumously" approving of the way things are being run..., all indications point to a second half-century of success for this "up-the-creek" and "under-the-redwoods" Big Sur hide-a-way...

As one continues south and away from the Big Sur valley's picturesque park and delightful diversions, the mighty Santa Lucias and the rugged Pacific shoreline again command the traveler's attention. In marveling at the mountains and their sheer drop into the sea, one can't help but wonder what it was like before man scarred the scene with dynamite and dump trucks as he built a monument to himself — and to a motorized public — in the form of magnificent Highway One.

Today there are relatively few old-timers who can remember the scene before this ribbon of cement linked the north with the south, and one must work fast if he wishes to record their recollections of the Big Sur coast. Other than old-timers and their treasure-trove of memories..., faded photographs, aged diaries, yellowed letters, forgotten newspapers, and a scattering of books are about all that is left for the historian to ponder.

It is this thought that brings us to our next tale, as it was an account from an aged newspaper (found in the scrapbook of a pioneer Monterey County resident) that brought to light the story of a crude south coast shack..., and a clock that wouldn't quit.

Recorded many years ago, the account tells of a 40-acre parcel of land — complete with cabin — that was being offered for sale. In hiking to the isolated acreage the teller of this tale told how, upon reaching the weathered cabin (located at a height of approximately 1,000 feet and a half-mile distance from the sea), both he and his partner were surprised at the way the Santa Lucia wilderness had "reclaimed" the land. Upon climbing over the remains of an old fence, the adventuresome pair cautiously continued through the overgrown yard to the entrance of the aged structure. On reaching the rickety steps leading to the dwelling's only door, they painstakingly unwound the rusted wire that held the door shut and entered the shack. As they crept into the long-vacant building they were startled to hear the sounds of a clock! Staring in bewilderment at the loudly ticking timepiece, the dumbfounded duo checked their watches against the aged clock..., and found — to their amazement — that they all recorded exactly the same time! Upon recovering from their initial shock, the astonished visitors spent the better part of an hour in and about the south coast shack..., satisfying themselves that the structure hadn't been entered for many years. Finally, upon taking their leave, they again checked the clock and found that not only was it ticking as loudly as ever..., but it was also keeping perfect time!

As they began their long trek away from the cabin, the somewhat shaken pair reported distinct and disturbing feelings of being watched. It was this information, related by the concerned hikers, that caused certain people to think of the often-told (and previously-discussed) tales of the Santa Lucia's mysterious dark watchers..., making them wonder if — for some unknown reason — these strange beings resided in the area of the lonely mountain shack, where they watched over (and wound) the aged alarm clock.

With thoughts such as these a bit difficult to accept, and with the mystery still unsolved as this work goes to press..., perhaps it is best to end this narrative with the information that (according to the scrapbook account), the cabin and its surrounding 40 acres were still for sale..., complete with the clock that refuses to stop...

As we near the southern extremities of the Big Sur coast, and as we come to the end of our collection of tales, one can't help but be impressed with the beauty of the area and the colorful part it has played in the history of the Golden State. Among the most interesting, and certainly one of the most important segments of this south coast history, is the fascinating story of Monterey County's remote Los Burros Mining District.

Formed in 1875, this "Monterey mother lode" of one hundred-plus years ago was somewhat typical of California's mining camps of Forty-Niner days. Prospectors combed the Santa Lucias, mines were claimed faster than they could be recorded, and a town sprang up in the heart of the district. In boasting such things as a one-room school, a post office, miners' cabins, a blacksmith shop, general stores, frontier hotels, a small cemetery, a dance hall and, of course, a full complement of saloons..., one can readily see that the mountain community of Manchester was a typical California mining town. Today Manchester is known as "The Lost City of the Santa Lucias", and can truly be considered a ghost of the past.

Other ghosts of Monterey County's "gold country" revolve around mysterious "Massacre Cave", where the skeletons of ten human beings were found..., and an equally mysterious "Headless Horselady", who roams the foothills of the Santa Lucias (most frequently in the vicinity of nearby Mission San Antonio) and who lost her life due to her involvement with a Los Burros prospector. (For those interested in learning more about the preceding accounts, the story of Massacre Cave is touched on in the author's book "GHOSTS, BANDITS AND LEGENDS of old Monterey" and is told in detail in his book "MONTEREY'S MOTHER LODE". The story of the Headless Horselady is recounted in his book "GHOSTLY TALES AND MYSTERIOUS HAPPENINGS of old Monterey".)

Other than a ghost town, a cave of death, and a headless horseback rider, there are several additional tales about Los Burros mines (and/or claims) that are of ghostly origin. Included in this category is the account of a claim that was duly recorded as "The Ghost of Gold". Mentioned in previous publications (including the Monterey Peninsula Herald newspaper), the story of this Los Burros mine has become a favorite of modern-day gold hunters.

In looking into the background of this Santa Lucia saga we find the claim to have been owned and worked by a woman. As if this isn't a bit strange on its own, the fact that this "miniature miner" boasted nearly two dozen additional claims in Monterey County's remote mining district, makes the story of even more interest. Holding her own and not pushed around by anyone, this mountain miss owned her own bulldozer as well as a jeep..., and when it came to hard work she put many of her fellow gold seekers to shame.

As to the Ghost of Gold and its mysterious haunts, our mining maiden told of having been frightened by strange and unnatural happenings in and around her south-coast holdings. In describing her experiences, she spoke somewhat hesitatingly of "earth-bound spirits" that frequented her ghost claim. In addition to ghostly spirits, she told of a strange wolf-like creature that had been observed around the mine, and of aged automobiles that were often heard — but never seen — as they chugged along the road and through the nearby trees.

With these sightings, feelings and sounds all being very real to our mountain maiden, and with the story having become fairly well known, several people have attempted to solve the mysteries with "logical" explanations. As to the sounds of the chugging automobiles, thoughts have been expressed that they were nothing more than the sounds of diesel-powered freighters that plied the waters of the distant Pacific. Because there are no wolves in Monterey County, the wolf, or wolf-like creature that was reported, has been described as a "possible" descendant of an escapee from the William Randolph Hearst zoo (of Hearst Castle fame) located in the extreme southern section of the Santa Lucia Mountains.

As logical, or illogical, as these explanations seem..., one must admit they are explanations, and they do offer somewhat simplified solutions to two of the Ghost of Gold's mysteries (however questionable the solutions may be). This brings us to the earth-bound spirits described by our lady miner, spirits that as yet have not been explained (at least to the author of this text). With no answers as to what the strange spirits may be, the fact that they were experienced — and were very real — to our Los Burros lass, makes them logical candidates for a long list of unanswered questions that pertain to the Los Burros area.

Among the many mysteries on this Los Burros list are the strange circumstances surrounding the disappearance of the district's first recorder of claims (who was last seen in 1907)..., and the equally mysterious disappearance of his son (the founder of the famed Last Chance Mine), thirty years later. If these two mysteries aren't enough to whet ones appetite and make him wonder..., perhaps a third mystery — one that involves a long-lost mine — will convince the reader that strange happenings abound in this remote mountain wilderness. Unrecorded and unknown, this ancient mine — boasting an arrow-straight hand-carved tunnel — was not discovered until the mid-1900s. To this day mining buffs and Los Burros veterans are amazed, and a bit confused, as to who the ghostly miners were who pointed their tunnel — from the back side — straight for the heart of the golden vein of the best paying mine in Monterey's mother lode...

SUMMARY

"INCREDIBLE GHOSTS of the BIG SUR COAST" is not meant to be the definitive work on strange and mysterious happenings as they pertain to this scenic stretch of California coastline. In a publication of this size and format it is only possible to "touch on" the colorful history and ghostly occurrences that are so much a part of this area. However, even though the book is small, it is the author's hope that the preceding tales have helped the reader become aware of the fascinating part Monterey County's "Big South" has played in the overall history of California's central coast.

Among the stories that have purposely been omitted are tales that, over the years, have become interesting and informative additions to the unique history of this wilderness region..., but stories which may also bring sad memories to pioneer families of the area. Not wanting to revive painful happenings which have long since taken place, the author chose to pass over these tales..., feeling it best to let the ghosts rest.

As to vouching for the book's authenticity, the author can only say that at times there is a fine line between fact and fiction, and sometimes the two overlap. When research was possible, the facts have been substantiated; however, when it comes to such things as ghostly sightings (and/or feelings) and unidentified objects, the author has only reported what was reported to him, leaving the final conclusions as to what is real, and what may have been imagined, up to the reader...